13 Art Illusions
Children Should Know

Silke Vry

PRESTEL

Munich · London · New York

Contents

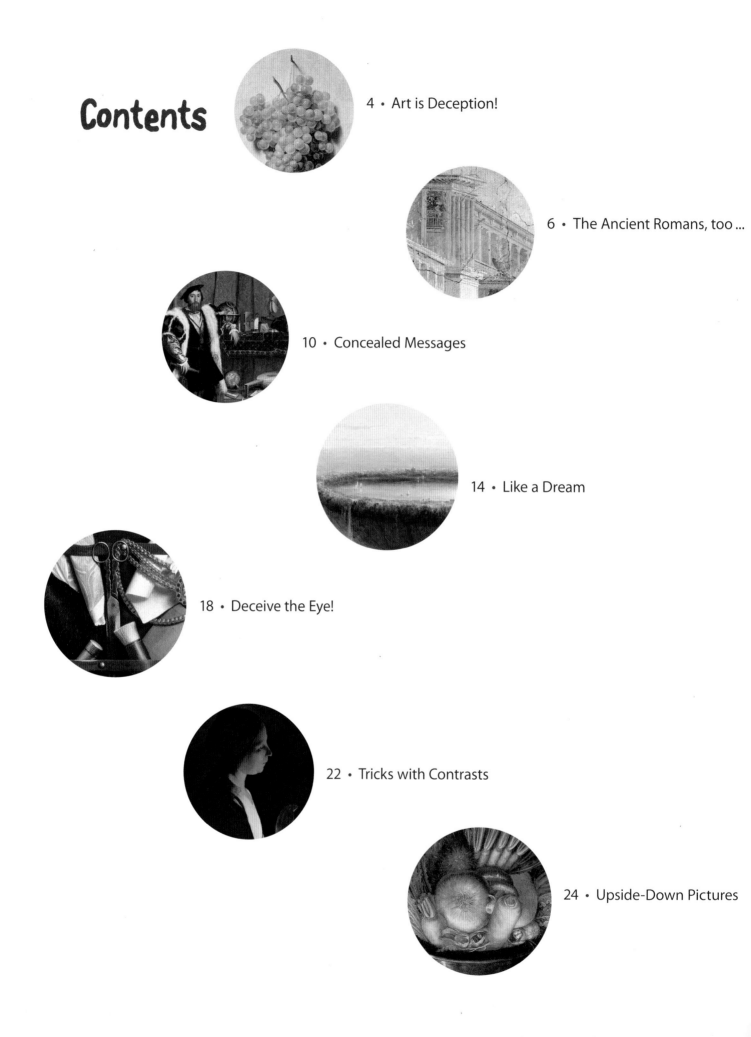

Artists are magicians and tricksters. They enchant and deceive us, and they lead us around by the nose. Their colors and forms fool our eyes, making us forget over and over again that their pictures are not real. But you don't need to fear the artist tricksters—for they do no harm. Instead, they promise fun, entertainment, and a glimpse into another world.

This book introduces you to thirteen *optical tricks*, or tricks of the eye, that artists use. Technical terms are marked with an asterisk* and are explained in the glossary on page 45. You'll find the answers to the quiz questions on page 46.

Have fun being fooled!

Technical terms are explained here.

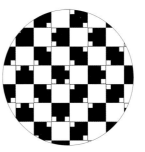

543 B.C. Beginning of the Buddhist calendar

600 B.C.	590	580	570	560	550	540	530	520	510	500	490

White Grapes,
Louis-Léopold Boilly,
1785–91, Musée des
Beaux-Arts, Rouen

Zeuxis' original paint-
ing—with its deceptively
realistic grapes—has
not survived. But it might
have looked something
like this.

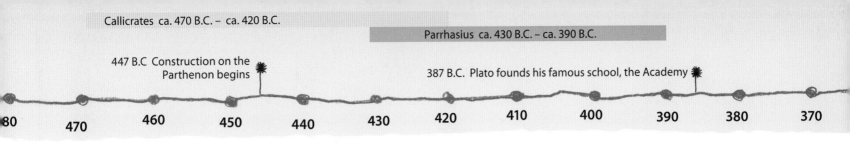

Art is Deception!

Even the ancient Greeks knew this motto, and they mastered the art of illusion more than 2,500 years ago.

One popular story from ancient Greece tells of two famous painters who wanted to prove their skills in a competition. One of them, Zeuxis, painted grapes that looked so delicious, pigeons actually tried to eat his "fruit"! But the other artist, Parrhasius, had painted even more carefully. He won the competition when his picture of a curtain fooled not just the animals, but even the people looking at it—who tried to draw the curtain aside to see the painting!

Works of ancient Greek architecture can also deceive. Do you think the columns of the Parthenon (shown here) stand up straight and the stairs are horizontal? Then you've been fooled. The magic here lies in the building's curvature. The Parthenon's architects knew that if they wanted these parts of the temple to look straight, they actually had to make them curved. This kind of optical* correction was invented as early as the sixth century B.C. A building without curvature would seem very rigid, stiff, and boring.

What:
  Optical deceptions and corrections in antiquity
When:
  Beginning around the 6th century B.C.
Who:
  Zeuxis, Parrhasius (painters); Ictinus, Callicrates (architects)
Where:
  Greece
Why:
  For painters: to imitate nature; For architects: to make buildings beautiful

Quiz question
If the "ball" on which the Parthenon stands was completed, it would have a diameter of roughly ...
a) 100 yards b) 400 yards
c) 6 miles
(Solution on page 46)

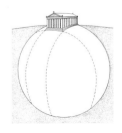

Parthenon,
fifth century B.C., Athens

The Parthenon on the Acropolis of Athens was built around 2,500 years ago. It stands on a curved surface, which is shaped like a section of a giant ball.

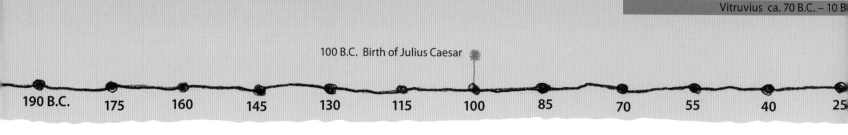

100 B.C. Birth of Julius Caesar

| 190 B.C. | 175 | 160 | 145 | 130 | 115 | 100 | 85 | 70 | 55 | 40 | 25 |

What:
   Roman (Pompeian) wall painting
When:
   Primarily the first century B.C. and first century A.D.
Where:
   Rome and southern Italy; the cities around Vesuvius (including Pompeii and Herculaneum) stand near the present-day city of Naples
Why:
   To make living spaces seem larger and more beautiful

The Ancient Romans, too ...

… knew a thing or two about the art of optical illusions.

Roman paintings were able to make small rooms seem like large, fantasy-filled spaces that appeared to open up into the endless distance. What did the Romans use to do this trick? Nothing more than paint, brushes, and a wall …

When the volcano Mount Vesuvius erupted in A.D. 79, its shower of ash buried many cities, houses, and inhabitants. More than 1,600 years later, people began to remove the thick ash layer left behind by the volcano. What was revealed, among other things, was the city of Pompeii. Excavators could scarcely believe their eyes: In the houses they discovered wall paintings that had been beautifully preserved through all the centuries, since they had been buried airtight beneath the earth for so long. These paintings showed that even in Roman times, people loved optical illusions that made their rooms appear larger.

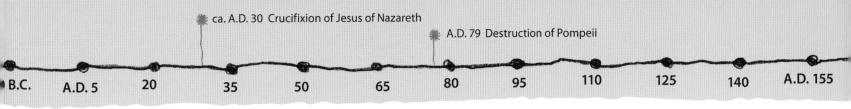

ca. A.D. 30 Crucifixion of Jesus of Nazareth

A.D. 79 Destruction of Pompeii

B.C.   A.D. 5   20   35   50   65   80   95   110   125   140   A.D. 155

Wall painting in the Villa Fannius, Boscoreale, ca. 40 B.C., Metropolitan Museum of Art, New York

The Villa Fannius was the country home of a noble family who had the walls painted with beautiful decorations. The town of Boscoreale is just north of Pompeii, and like Pompeii it was buried by the eruption of Mount Vesuvius.

Unswept Floor,
second century A.D.,
mosaic from a villa on
the Aventine Hill,
Vatican Museum, Rome

Sitting on a floor like
this during a meal was
both fun and practical!
Anything that might
accidentally fall on the
floor could "disappear"
among all the other
realistic-looking food
debris. The floor is
actually a mosaic—a
picture made of tiny
pieces of colored
stone and glass.

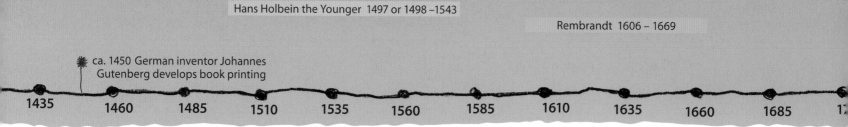
The Ambassadors,
Hans Holbein the
Younger, 1533, National
Gallery, London

"Remember that you shall
die!": In art, the skull is
often used as a symbol of
the transience of life. In
order not to frighten the
viewer, the painter of this
picture has hidden the
skull.

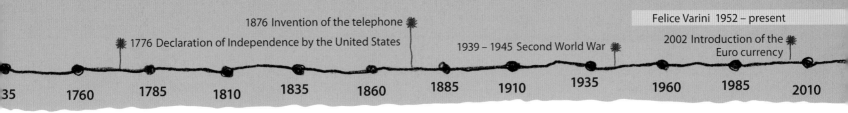

1876 Invention of the telephone

1776 Declaration of Independence by the United States

1939 – 1945 Second World War

Felice Varini 1952 – present

2002 Introduction of the Euro currency

35   1760   1785   1810   1835   1860   1885   1910   1935   1960   1985   2010

Concealed Messages

Sometimes entire messages are hidden in pictures—hidden so well that you might miss them even when they're right before your eyes.

What:
Anamorphoses ("transfigurations"), distortions on paintings

When:
Primarily in the 17th and 18th centuries

Why:
First as a means of hiding messages in pictures, later for fun

Here we see two serious-looking men. Between them are books, musical instruments, and mathematical objects that look so real, even the smallest detail can be detected. It almost appears as if the objects were physically lying in front of us. And one more thing makes the image seem so lifelike: It is enormous in size, over six feet (two meters) high and wide. In fact, the painted men are the size of real people! They look directly out at us, almost as if we're in the same room with them.

But if you inspect the picture more closely, an optical illusion enters the scene: A strange form appears in the front center. But what on earth does the form represent?

In order to solve this puzzle, there's one thing you need to know: The strange form is an anamorphosis*, a distortion of perspective* that can be clearly seen only when it is "straightened out". To do this, you need to view the picture in a foreshortened way—that is, by standing in a specific place and looking at the image from the correct vantage point. To help you find the vantage point here, look for the white arrow, view the picture from that angle (with your nose directly against the paper), and the mysterious form

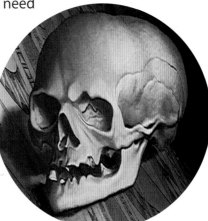

This painting probably once hung in a staircase, so that from the stairs the viewer could see the skull clearly, without distortion.

will appear: a skull! Hans Holbein may have painted the skull to tell his viewers that life is short—a message only revealed if one knows how to find it.

11

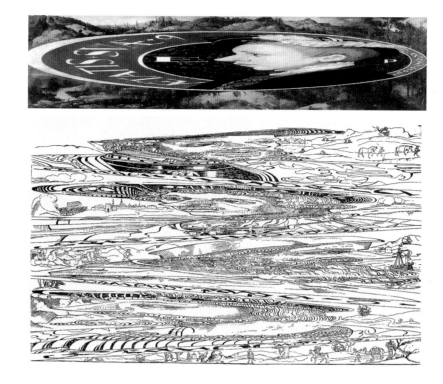

Look at these two pictures by placing your nose sideways against the book and glancing at one picture after the other, one eye at a time. What is hidden there?

Is this a painted dream? A dreamed painting? You might ask yourself these questions when you look at the anamorphoses* in the right way.

Whoever enters a room with walls painted like these is sure of one thing: This artwork is no *Mona Lisa*. The *Mona Lisa* (and almost all other pictures) can be looked at and recognized from any vantage point. But when you come across a "picture" like this, you first have to look for—and hopefully find—the perfect standpoint. Then you can view the distorted areas in such a way that they look perfectly "normal".

Four Planes of a Rectangle,
Felice Varini, 2007, exhibition *Une saison Suisse* in the Musée des Beaux-Arts d'Arras

As you can see here, the artist did not paint a real circle. Instead, he made warped surfaces of color.

**Four Planes
of a Rectangle,**
Felice Varini, 2007,
exhibition *Une saison
Suisse* in the Musée des
Beaux-Arts d'Arras

Only when they're seen
from a specific point in
space do the painted
surfaces form circles.
But how was Felice Varini
able to do this trick so
well? Quite simply, he
drew the circles before-
hand and projected them
onto the walls with a slide
projector. His picture
then became distorted,
and he very carefully
copied these distortions
on the walls.

**Show this illustration
to your friends and
ask if one of them can
guess how the optical
illusion is made. You
can then show them the
solution in the photo at
left.**

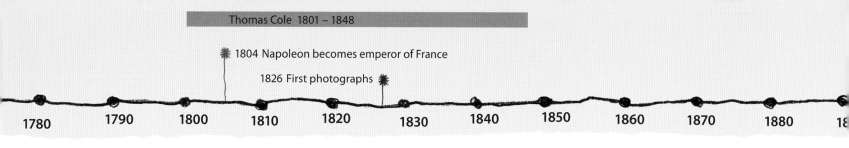

The Titian's Goblet,
Thomas Cole, 1833,
Metropolitan Museum
of Art, New York

Do the people on these
ships suspect that there
is a world beyond their
goblet? Surely not!
Otherwise, why would
they sail so carelessly
across the water?

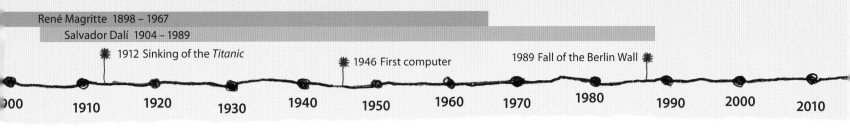

René Magritte 1898 – 1967
Salvador Dalí 1904 – 1989

✴ 1912 Sinking of the *Titanic*

✴ 1946 First computer

1989 Fall of the Berlin Wall ✴

900   1910   1920   1930   1940   1950   1960   1970   1980   1990   2000   2010

Like a Dream ...

Painters hold great power over us. Their pictures can bewilder our senses and make us believe that we're not in the real world but in a dream ...

What:
Surrealism: Pictures that bewilder the senses
When:
Primarily in the 20th century
Why:
To turn reality upside-down

As in this picture: How gigantic must this cup be if boats can sail around in it and houses can stand along its rim? And why do we believe this illusion when we know that a real goblet is only about the size of a flower vase? For the simple reason that we make a comparison with our eyes, and we come to the only conclusion that seems to make sense: It's not the ships, houses, and mountains that are miniscule, but the cup that's enormous. This is because a strange object is often more "logical" to our eyes than a tiny landscape. When we first look at an optical illusion, it seems real to us and we believe what we see in it. After a short time, however, our better judgment tells us that the illusion can't really be true!

The painter René Magritte understood one thing better than almost anyone else—that common, everyday objects can be painted in ways that surprise people over and over again. Magritte's paintings always represent things in great detail. But at the same time they defy our expectations, differing from what we trust and find familiar. Where, for example, is this lady riding? Is she in front of the trees, behind the trees, or between them? And what's going on in this "ordinary" room that makes it seem so puzzling and so strange? Magritte was part of an art movement called Surrealism*, in which painters sought to depict things that were dreamlike and fantastical—and to make these things appear in their own separate reality.

Personal Values,
René Magritte, 1952,
Museum of Modern Art,
San Francisco

A glass that appears
enormous next to
a normal-sized bed
confuses our senses
and unsettles us.

Carte Blanche,
René Magritte, 1965,
National Gallery of Art,
Washington, D.C.

We're just as bewildered by a person whose location we can't exactly pin down. We take what we see to be real, but we can't explain what we see here.

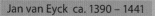
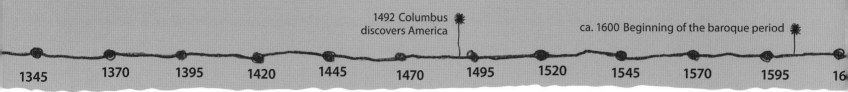
Escaping Criticism,
Borrell de Caso, 1874,
Banco de España
Collection, Madrid

This picture was
originally called
"An Impossible Thing."
And that's exactly
what it is! For how
can a painted boy
leave his own
painting?

nuel van Hoogstraten 1627 – 1678

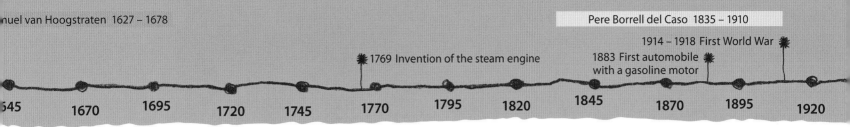

Pere Borrell del Caso 1835 – 1910

1914 – 1918 First World War

1883 First automobile
with a gasoline motor

1769 Invention of the steam engine

645   1670   1695   1720   1745   1770   1795   1820   1845   1870   1895   1920

Deceive the Eye!

Some pictures look so realistic that they are called
tromp l'oeil—which is French for "to deceive the eye."

Deception was the goal of many painters in the past. They specifically
set out to trick their viewer's eyes, and their flat pictures often made us
believe we were looking at people and spaces in the real world.

For example, we are startled when we look at an image like this: A boy is
leaving the dark picture space of his own painting! How can this be?
He's only painted, isn't he? Yet he's already got one foot on the golden
picture frame; and he's holding on tight with his hands, about to pull
himself right out of the scene.

But why are our eyes fooled by this image? Have we overlooked something that makes this illusion of a living boy so perfect, something
other than his realistic skin and lifelike eyes?

But of course! We simply have to ask our-
selves, "How can a painted boy cast a shadow
on a picture frame, or even grab hold of it
and step on it?"

Only when that realistic-looking frame
is itself a painted image ...

What:
Tromp l'oeil, art that
deceives the eye
When:
During antiquity,
and then again since
the Renaissance and
baroque eras
Why:
For amusement

**Portrait of a Man with
a Carnation,**
Jan van Eyck (or follower),
ca. 1435, Gemäldegalerie
Berlin

An older man looks out at
us almost as if he's about to
speak. To make us believe
this, not only did the artist
paint everything in great
detail, but he also made use
of a little trick.

Quodlibet*,
Samuel van Hoogstraten,
1666–78, Staatliche
Kunsthalle Karlsruhe

A comb, a feather, and
much more—what looks
like an old-fashioned
"bulletin board" turns out
to be a painting: a quod-
libet*. When you look
more closely at it, you can
discover even more: the
painting tells us some-
thing about the painter,
his preferences, and his
hobbies.

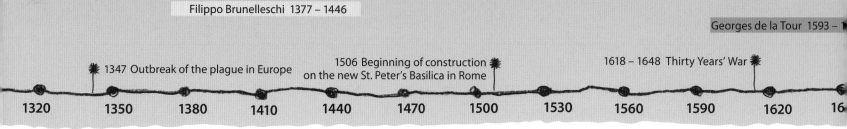

Filippo Brunelleschi 1377 – 1446

Georges de la Tour 1593 – 1

✳ 1347 Outbreak of the plague in Europe   1506 Beginning of construction ✳
on the new St. Peter's Basilica in Rome   1618 – 1648 Thirty Years' War ✳

1320   1350   1380   1410   1440   1470   1500   1530   1560   1590   1620   16

What:
  Chiaroscuro
Why:
  To emphasize specific
  areas of an image
  and make others
  recede into the back-
  ground
When:
  Since the 14th century

Tricks with Contrasts

With light colors you can paint a bright and friendly picture. Dark colors, on the other hand, create a more somber one. But by using light and dark together, astonishing things can happen ...

In order to make something that's easily readable or easily visible, one needs to write or draw with contrasting* colors—light colors against a dark surface or dark colors against a light surface. Using colors that are similarly light or dark makes everything seem to blend together. Nothing is able to stand out. Anyone who has painted or drawn knows that a dark-light contrast, or chiaroscuro, gives things plasticity*, since dark colors seem to recede and light ones seem to push forward optically. Light tones draw our attention more than dark ones. So when light-colored people and objects are painted on a dark background, they often appear to "jump out" of the picture.

a) A yellow banana on a yellow ground: They almost merge together.
b) As soon as the surrounding color is darker, it's easier to see the banana ...
c) And as soon as the background is completely black, the banana begins to glow ...

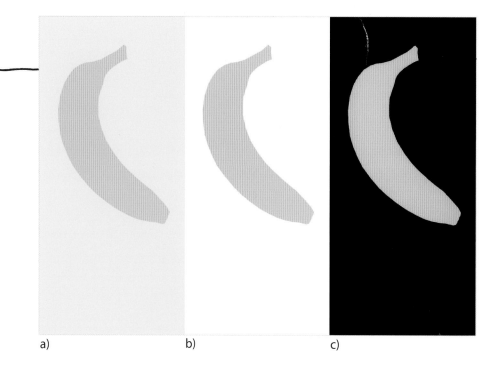

a)   b)   c)

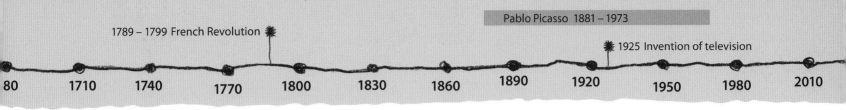
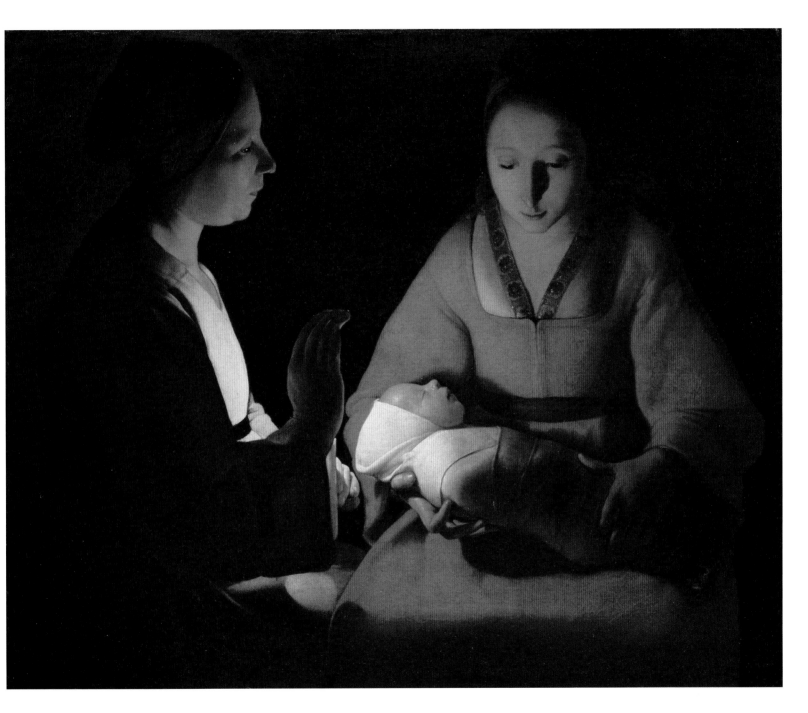

The Newborn Christ,
Georges de la Tour, 1645–48, Musee des Beaux Arts, Rennes

The woman on the left holds a candle and protects the flame from the wind with her hand. The candlelight illuminates the two women and the baby, making them seem to glow amid the darkness.

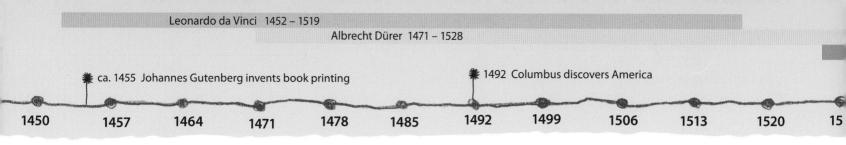
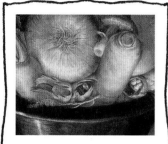

What:
The negative image, the upside-down image, and the disguised face—pictures hidden in pictures

Who:
Giuseppe Arcimboldo is the most famous artist of the hidden image

Why:
For amusement

Upside-Down Pictures

Here we find a picture on its head. Even without turning it over, it's easy to identify the painting: It's the *Mona Lisa* by Leonardo da Vinci, the most famous picture in the world.

Oops, what's this?! As soon as we turn her over, the lady looks different than we expected! How is this possible?

The answer is simple: When we look at a picture, it's not possible for us to imagine it upside down at the same time. Objects that we would recognize immediately when they're right-side-up can often remain hidden or altered when they're shown upside-down.

Some painters have made use of this optical phenomenon. They've hidden entire images in their pictures, which the viewer only discovers when the whole image is turned upside-down. What looks like a basket of fruit can become something completely different when it's turned around.

What do you think these drawings will look like when they're shown upside-down? Can you guess the answer before you turn them over?

24

The Vegetable Gardener,
Giuseppe Arcimboldo,
second half of the
16th century, Museo
Civico, Cremona

The Italian Renaissance
painter Giuseppe
Arcimboldo is famous for
his "hidden" heads. He
composes these heads
out of pieces of fruit.
Turn the painting upside
down to see the head!

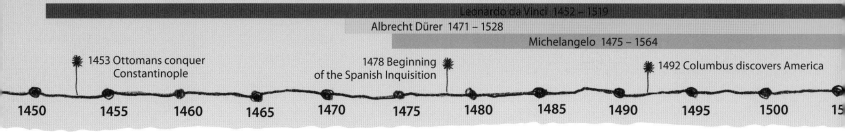

Leonardo da Vinci 1452 – 1519

Albrecht Dürer 1471 – 1528

Michelangelo 1475 – 1564

1453 Ottomans conquer
Constantinople

1478 Beginning
of the Spanish Inquisition

1492 Columbus discovers America

1450   1455   1460   1465   1470   1475   1480   1485   1490   1495   1500   15

Landscape near Romanel,
Félix Vallotton, 1900, private collection

Atmospheric perspective can make landscape paintings look remarkably realistic. By using more intense colors for the foreground and less intense colors for the background, artists can give their landscapes the illusion of vast space. Here, the painter has depicted a hilly scene at sunset. So he has used reddish tones for the background rather than bluish ones.

🌲 1517 Martin Luther hangs up his *Ninety-Five Theses*, helping begin Christianity's Protestant Reformation

Atmospheric Perspective

In landscape paintings you can usually tell what's closer and what's farther away. How do painters do this? By using a trick called *atmospheric perspective*.

If you look at an object from up close, you can easily perceive how big it is. Yet the farther away you get from the object, the smaller it seems to be—even though it hasn't really decreased in size. This is a simple rule of perspective*, something that we observe all the time.

But objects don't merely become smaller and smaller as they get farther away. They also change their color, a natural phenomenon that Leonardo da Vinci described when he wrote, "There is a kind of perspective called atmospheric perspective that depends on differences in the density of the air. Seen through dense air every object appears bluish, as you can see for example in the case of mountains. Objects farther from the eye appear smaller than they really are, and since there is a lot of air in between the appearance of the objects is less intense." Even today painters still use softer, less "intense" colors for their backgrounds when they want to make landscapes appear naturalistic.

What:
Atmospheric perspective and color perspective
How:
By using blue and other less intense colors in the background
Who:
First described by Leonardo
Why:
To generate the illusion of depth

You can reproduce the same phenomenon by means of a little experiment. You'll need a large glass container filled with water—a flower vase, for example —as well as a few drops of milk (very little!) and a flashlight.
Add the drops of milk to the water. Then shine the flashlight from above against the glass and observe the light falling through the water from the side. You should see the light as a bluish shimmer, similar to the blue of the sky in atmospheric perspective.

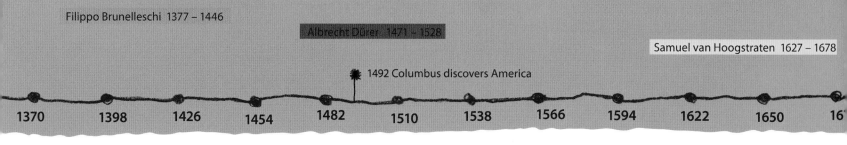

What:
  Perspective*
Who:
  Figured out by
  Filippo Brunelleschi*
Why:
  To represent space
  realistically, to play
  with perspective

Pictures with Depth

Artists have long painted rooms, rows of houses, and views of cities that seem to recede into the distance. All of them had learned the rules of linear perspective.

You can learn about linear perspective by drawing a cube in two different ways. Try it yourself using the illustration below. Cube "a" is drawn with "parallel projection", meaning that the lines of the cube remain parallel to one another as they extend into the distance.

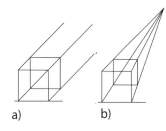

a)   b)

But cube "b" is drawn using linear perspective, so that the receding lines appear to merge together at a single imagined "vanishing point". This trick makes cube "b" appear to go farther back into space than cube "a". Painters use linear perspective to create a similar sense of depth in their artworks.

Woodcut from *Four Books on Measurement*, Albrecht Dürer, 1525

German artist Albrecht Dürer described the basic rules of perspective in 1525. At the time, people were convinced that this knowledge was essential for an artist.

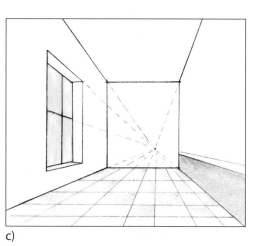

c)

Corridor,
Samuel van Hoogstraten,
1662, Dyrham Park, Avon

A dog looks out at us,
and even the house cat
seems to be waiting for
everyone to come in.
What has the artist done
to make us believe that
we're looking into the
deep space of a house?

Relativity,
M. C. Escher, 1953,
National Gallery of Art,
Washington, D.C.

M. C. Escher painted and
drew pictures that were
known for their optical
illusions and their "impossible" constructions. His
pictures made possible
things that would never
have existed in reality,
as this drawing of an
"unending" staircase
shows.

People who master the rules of perspective can also bend and play with
those rules. They can create pictures with carefully "built-in" mistakes that
cause confusion and amusement. These two artists were especially good
at doing such tricks.

Satire on False Perspective,
William Hogarth, 1754,
British Museum,
London

"Whoever makes a design without the knowledge of perspective will be liable to such absurdities as are shewn in this frontispiece." W. Hogarth

Quiz question
Can you find the places in this picture that are especially confusing and can only exist on paper?
(Solution on page 46)

Michelangelo Buonarroti 1475 – 1564

Andrea Palladio 1508 – 1580

✺ 1478 Beginning of the
Spanish Inquisition

✺ 1506 Construction begins on the new St. Peter's Basilica in Rome

1460   1470   1480   1490   1500   1510   1520   1530   1540   1550   1560   15

Teatro Olimpico,
Andrea Palladio, 1580–1585, Vicenza

This theater is a spectacle in its own right: The floor
rises up, the sky comes down to meet it, and the statues
in the niches become smaller in the distance. Very short
actors used to play out scenes in the background, so as
to intensify the feeling that the stage was a vast, deep
space.

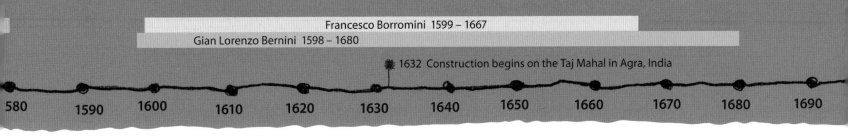
Built Illusions

"I would love to have more space!" … Most of us have felt this way about our own homes.

In art, things aren't always as they appear. This is true of architecture as well as painting. With a few tricks, any room can be enlarged visually without making the space actually bigger.

Many architects mastered these tricks during the Renaissance and baroque periods. Their squares, hallways, staircases, and theaters often surprised visitors, for they looked much grander than they actually were. Great architects like Michelangelo, Bernini, Palladio, and Borromini achieved almost incredible effects with their built illusions. In Palladio's Teatro Olimpico, which is shown here, it looks like there's a whole city behind the stage. But in reality the space is only a couple of yards (or meters) deep. The trick: The structures on the stage are built a little bit smaller the farther back they go. This technique fools our eyes, since we know intuitively that things which are the same size have to look smaller when they're farther away.

What:
Architectural tromp l'oeil, distortions of perspective

When:
Primarily during the late Renaissance and baroque eras

Why:
To create the illusion of size and distance in a restricted space

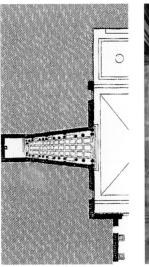

a)

b)

Galleria Spada,
Francesco Borromini,
17th century, Rome

In Borromini's architectural illusion, the distance to the last column looks much farther than it actually is. Why? The columns become smaller as they recede, not only optically but also in reality. Even once you know this, you're still taken in by the trick!

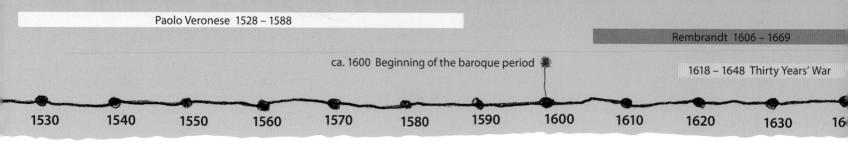

What:
Mock architecture

When:
Primarily in the baroque era

Where:
In churches and palaces with high ceilings and large walls

Why:
To give the illusion of spatial depth, to "open up" a room visually

Mock Architecture

What the ancient Romans wanted so long ago (see page 6), later people wanted as well—to "see through" solid walls and look out onto endless vistas!

During the Renaissance, artists began to rediscover ancient tricks with brush and paint, transforming their houses and churches. These painters used the rules of perspective to make it seem like the physical room continued onto the painted surface. Such illusions worked especially well on high ceilings, where it was hard to tell the difference between what was painted and what wasn't. For this reason, many church ceilings were painted with an open sky populated by angels and other figures. Such illusions also worked effectively in the large halls of palaces and villas.

Young Woman and Maidservant,
Paolo Veronese, ca. 1560, Villa Barbaro, Maser

If you think you can walk through this villa unobserved, guess again. There are people watching all over the place. Even though they're silent and "only" painted, they look very alert and probably don't miss a thing!

Girl Opening a Door,
Paolo Veronese,
ca. 1560, Villa
Barbaro, Maser

A little girl peeks
curiously through the
door. Up close it's easy
to see that she's painted,
but from a distance
the painting looks
deceptively real.

**Marble Hall
in Melk Abbey,**
Paul Troger, Gaetano
Fanti, 1731–32, Melk,
Austria

Any of the guests who
once celebrated in this
ballroom got a thrill
when they happened
to look upwards. The
ceiling opened up
directly above them,
and in the blue "sky" the
Greek goddess Athena
and the hero Hercules
floated downwards to
welcome them.

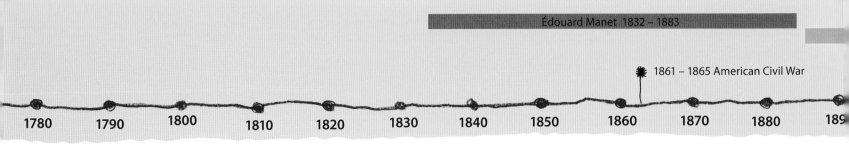

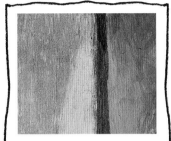

What:
Complementary colors, simultaneous contrast

Who:
Modern painters

When:
Used intentionally since the 19th century

Why:
To intensify the effects or color

Colors Do the Trick

Every artist who paints with colors knows that they can perform wonderful tricks.

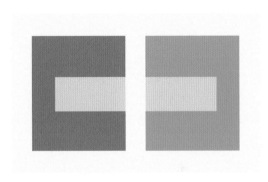

Both of these blue-green bars are absolutely the same, but the one against the blue background looks greener and the one against the green background looks bluer. The one on the left also seems warmer.

For a painter, this phenomenon means that colors on a canvas don't always look the same as when they come out of the paint tube. If an artist wants to paint the same bluish-green pillow twice in one picture—once on a blue chair and once on a green sofa—he can't use the same color each time. For the pillows to look exactly the same, he has to use two slightly different colors.

Modern painters have known how colors "functioned", and they've understood how to choose specific combinations to increase the brilliance of individual hues. By placing complementary* colors together—yellow next to purple, blue next to orange, or red next to green—they can make these colors really glow. Take a look at the picture on the facing page. It shows a scene in the bright light of northern Africa. The painter wanted to make it glow intensely, so he used the pairs of colors that we just listed. Can you find them?

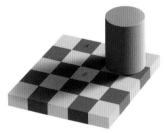

Even black, white, and gray can play tricks on our eyes. Prove it to yourself: Which field is darker, A or B?

ust Macke 1887 – 1914

Andy Warhol 1928 – 1987

2001 Terror attack on the World Trade Center in New York City

1969 First moon landing

1933 Adolf Hitler rises to power in Germany

1900   1910   1920   1930   1940   1950   1960   1970   1980   1990   2000   2010

Turkish Cafe,
August Macke, 1914,
Lenbachhaus, Munich

During his trip to the city of Tunis in Tunisia, August Macke painted incredibly bright pictures. He was inspired by the area's natural colors, which seemed especially brilliant under the blazing African sun. But Macke also did something else: By combining specific colors on a single painting (red and green; purple and yellow), he made the colors look even more intense.

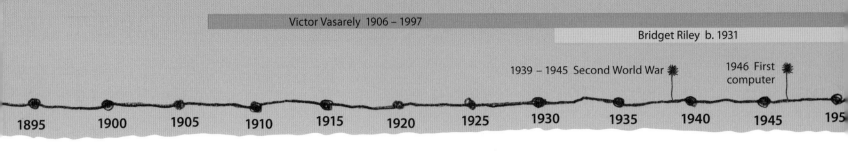

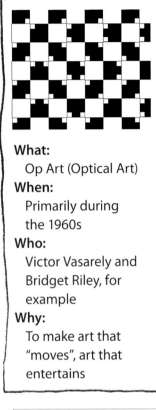

What:
  Op Art (Optical Art)
When:
  Primarily during
  the 1960s
Who:
  Victor Vasarely and
  Bridget Riley, for
  example
Why:
  To make art that
  "moves", art that
  entertains

Moving Pictures

Around fifty years ago, a few artists began to paint pictures that looked like they were moving, turning, or leading into the distance.

They didn't need a lot to achieve this effect. Many of their artworks used simple geometric patterns and a limited number of colors—sometimes just black and white. Yet the artists were able to create remarkable illusions with these simple means. Optical Art, or Op Art, was the name given to such works. Their energetic quality reflected the people of the time, who wanted nothing more than to be on the move, constantly changing and entertaining.

The picture *Rotating Snakes* by Akiyoshi Kitaoka appears on the cover of this book, and it is a perfect example of Op Art. Its apparent movement is only an illusion, of course. Such movement occurs because the brain forms so-called afterimages of what it has just seen. These illusions, which appear in colors that are complimentary* to those on the canvas, become mixed together with the actual image. You can see for yourself how afterimages arise: Keep your eyes fixed on sheet 1 for about a minute, then look at the white area next to it. What do you see? You can try the same thing with the other sheets.

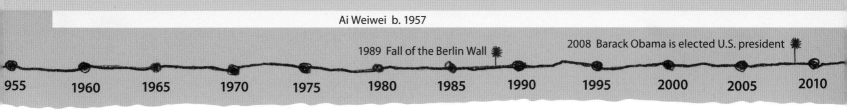

Zebra,
Victor Vasarely, 1944,
private collection

Victor Vasarely's first great work showed two zebras. With this picture, he became the founder of a new art movement called Op Art*. Zebras were main subject in several of Vasarely's paintings.

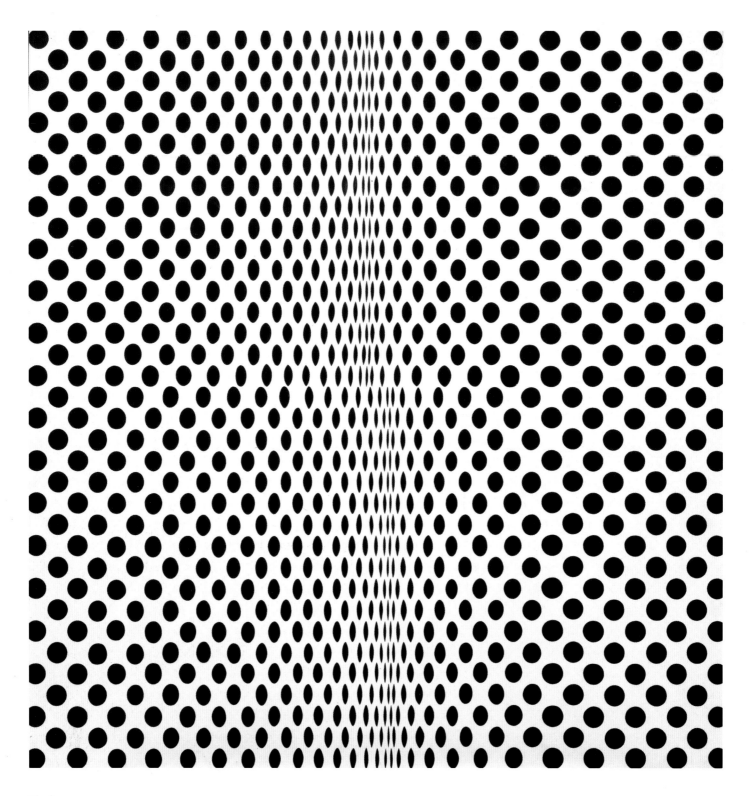

Fission,
Bridget Riley, 1963, Museum
of Modern Art, New York

Our eyes can be tricked with the
simplest of devices. Even black dots
on a white background are enough.
It all depends on their size and
arrangement ...

Cataract III,
Bridget Riley, 1967, British Council Collection,
London

Bridget Riley's pictures seem to burst forth from
their flat canvases—or to carry them off in their
energetic momentum. But if you actually touch the
painted surface, you'll know better. All of the waves
and bulges are perfectly flat and perfectly still.

Here you can try your hand at an Op Art picture yourself: Color in all the fields with black dots. Be careful not to color over the light lines. What do you notice when you look at your finished artwork?

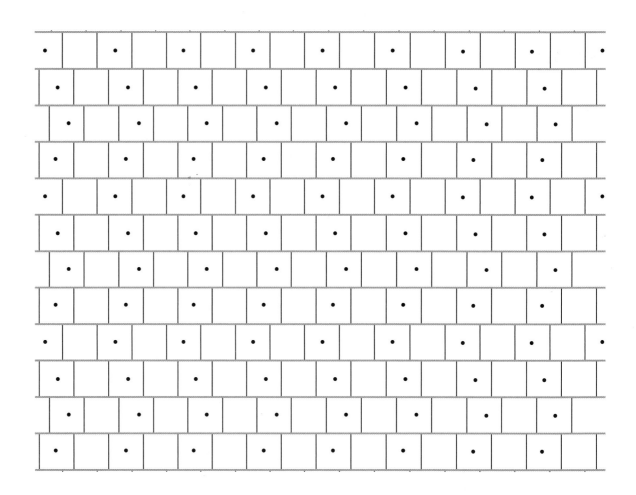

This picture seems to be moving. But why? We see nothing other than round blue circles on a green background. Each circle is surrounded by a white and a black crescent shape, arranged in different ways. And herein lies the trick: we interpret black as "shadow" and white as "light." Without our thinking about it our brains conclude that some of the blue circles are holding one side towards the light, and the other ones the other side, that they're positioned differently, that is. Our brain's "explanation" is that the surface is in motion!

Glossary

ANAMORPHOSIS comes from the Greek word for "transformation" or "reshaping". Painters use this technique to make objects appear distorted in precise ways. The objects become "straightened out" when the viewer looks at the picture from a certain vantage point, usually from the side. An anamorphosis can be a whole picture or just part of it. Artists who paint anamorphoses have mastered the rules of perspective*.

FILIPPO BRUNELLESCHI, 1377–1446, was an Italian architect, engineer, and sculptor. He is considered a discoverer of perspective in architecture. With the help of an optical instrument of his own invention, he painted a picture of Florence's cathedral square in which the buildings appear to recede "naturally" into space.

COMPLEMENTARY COLORS. When they are mixed together as colored light, complementary colors always produce white. One can produce the complement of a primary color—red, yellow, or blue—by mixing the two other primary colors. Thus red's complimentary color is green, the mixture of blue and yellow. Placing two complementary colors next to each other can lead to optical effects such as flickering.

CONTRAST comes from the Latin words *contra* (against) and *stare* (to stand). In art, contrast refers to the difference between colors, especially between dark and light.

OP-ART, short for Optical Art, is an art movement that began in the mid-1900s. By using specific colors and patterns, Op Artists created flickering effects that made the painted surface appear to be moving.

OPTICS, from the Greek word *optike* ("the science of the visible"), refers to anything having to do with sight. In physics, it is the science of the movement of light.

PERSPECTIVE comes from the Latin word *perspicere*, which means "to inspect". Many artists have used perspective to represent space and the objects within it (houses, streets, squares, etc.). Their artworks have the illusion of depth—making viewers feel like they are "looking into" the two-dimensional pictures.

PLASTICITY means to depict the volume, or three-dimensional shape, of a painted object. An object painted plastically looks convincingly real and sculptural.

QUODLIBET, from the Latin term for "something fancied", is a specific form of still life. It consists of a group of every-day objects painted in a precise and deceptively real way.

SURREALISM, an important movement in modern art, sought to represent the dreamlike and the non-real. In 1924, several artists formed a group that founded the Surrealist movement.

Answers to the Quiz Questions

p. 5:   c) 6 miles!

p. 12:   When you look at these pictures from the side, you can discover various portraits.

p. 31:

p. 38:   Fields A and B are exactly the same shade, even if we feel certain that field A is darker.

© Prestel Verlag, Munich · London · New York, 2012
© for the reproduced works held by the artists, their heirs, or successors, with the exception of René Magritte, Felice Varini, Victor Vasarely: © VG Bild-Kunst, Bonn 2012; M.C. Escher: © 2012 The M.C. Escher Company-Holland. All rights reserved. www.mcescher.com; Bridget Riley: © Bridget Riley 2012. All rights reserved, courtesy Karsten Schubert, London; Akiyoshi Kitaoka: © Akiyoshi Kitaoka 2003, © KANZEN

Die Deutsche Nationalbibliothek lists this publication in the Deutsche Nationalbibliografie; detailed bibliographic information can be found at http://dnb.d-nb.de.

Front cover: Akiyoshi Kitaoka: *Rotating Snakes*, 2003 (see p. 40)
Back cover: Louis-Léopold Boilly: *White Grapes* (see p. 4); Giuseppe Arcimboldo: *The Vegetable Gardener* (see p. 25); Paolo Veronese: *Girl Opening a Door* (see p. 35)
Frontispiece: Laurent Dabos: *Traite Definitif de Paix*, trompe l'oeil on the subject of the restitution of Louisiana to France , 1801

Photo credits:
Sources for the reproductions are from the archive of the publisher with the exception of p. 12, p. 13: ADAGP; p. 4 and detail p. 2 and p. 5: Artothek; p. 36–37: Getty Images; p. 43: Courtesy Karsten Schubert, London; p. 30: The M.C. Escher Company Holland; p. 42: Scala; p. 32 and detail p. 3 and p. 33, p. 33 right: Ullstein Bild

Prestel Verlag, Munich
Verlagsgruppe Random House GmbH
www.prestel.com

Project direction: Doris Kutschbach
Image editing: Andrea Jaroni
Copyediting: Brad Finger
Translation: Cynthia Hall
Design: Michael Schmölzl, agenten.und.freunde. Munich
Art Direction: Cilly Klotz
Layout: Meike Sellier, Eching
Production: Astrid Wedemeyer
Lithography: ReproLine Mediateam, Munich
Printing and binding: Printer Trento, Trento

Verlagsgruppe Random House FSC-DEU-0100
The FSC®-certified paper *Eurobulk* has been supplied by Paper Union.

ISBN 978-3-7913-7110-8